I0390391

# Could You Lose Your Land To The Government?

*Protecting Your Property From Most Government Repossession Methods*

*Teresa Fikes*

By reading this document, the reader agrees that under no circumstances are we responsible for any losses, direct or indirect, which are incurred as a result of the use of information contained within this document, including, but not limited to, —errors, omissions, or inaccuracies.

**ISBN:** 9781098918262
**Imprint:** Independently published

# Table Of Contents

# Introduction

When all is said and done and you've prepped your homestead to the best of your abilities, your worries are supposed to relate to keeping yourself and your family safe, as well as maintaining food, water, and resources through various methods described in this website.

What you shouldn't have to worry about — but ultimately do — is the sensitive subject of the United States government repossessing your land.

There are five predominant ways that the government could go about taking your land. We're going to cover the following subject material listed below, including highlights of the fine print.

- Eminent Domain

- Surface Rights

- Air Rights

- Real Property

- Mineral Rights

There are also other ways in which your land can be taken. We'll show some examples, but they're not to be taken lightly:

- Condemnation

- Memorial Condemnation

- Taxruptcy

At the end of this book, you'll know the degrees in which you can protect your property from most government repossession methods, which would otherwise encroach on your rights as a home and landowner.

# Chapter 1: Eminent Domain

*"The right of a government or its agent to expropriate private property for public use, with payment of compensation."*
*– Oxford Dictionary*

It's the Fifth Amendment right for the government to seize property in its exercise of eminent domain, and our fourteenth amendment right to just compensation for their use of our land. But in an SHTF scenario, it's he who swings the bigger stick that claims the equivalent of the Fifth Amendment. We're all aware of the possibility of strong factions banding together in unison, and no law is going to protect us from such an incident.

In the case of a post-collapse world, will the government still hold reign? You'd be foolish to think they'd fall to pieces. If the dollar crashes and burns, government agents, no matter what level, would side with the guys in charge of the military. Money loses value; protection becomes a hot commodity along from food and water.

An agency can come through and claim eminent domain in the case that your wind turbines, rainwater harvesters, and farms are all in good condition. For the benefit of the people, they may say, and what can you do but step aside? Under the circumstances of a pickup full of gunned men arriving, you'd be smart to hand over your property with the declaration of your fourteenth amendment rights.

In the event that this happens prior to a fractured, end-of-the-world society, here's what you can do to avoid them taking: deny them.

In a court of law, your homestead may be seen as a resource more than a home. Pipeline requests under the guise of eminent domain have been fought in the past for less. Why shouldn't you get your day in court with the government? It is arguably the best line of defense.

*Note: If you are called upon in court to contest the actions of the government, be certain to consult a legal team of certified lawyers before continuing.*

# Chapter 2: Surface Rights

*"The set of rights associated with the surface of the land only, as differentiated from mineral rights."*
*– mineralweb.com*

This is sort of a split on mineral rights, which we'll learn about at the end of this little guide. Surface right pertains to everything above ground, which means the ground itself. If somebody else owns the mineral rights to your land (subterranean minerals and resources) they would have to pass onto your land in order to acquire them.

In this case, they would owe you, at the very least, constant contact and knowledge about what exactly was going on. In some cases, you can charge them to use your surface rights to access their mineral rights.

In *The Beverly Hillbillies*, Jed Clampett wouldn't have made a dime if he didn't possess both the surface rights and the mineral rights, as would have been declared on the deed. It's something of note.

Check the deed to your homestead to know what's inclusive and what's missing. You could be at risk for government land repossession under extreme circumstances.

# Chapter 3: Air Rights

*"Right to control, occupy or use the vertical space (air space) above a property subject to necessary and reasonable use by a neighbor(s) and others (such as an aircraft.)"*
*– businessdictionary.com*

To get a fully comprehensive guide on the definition of Air Rights, view the video below.

You own the air rights to your property; that is a given. Whatever the diameter of your actual property is, it extends to essentially infinity. While you can't charge United Airlines for using your airspace 30,000 feet above, you can be in the big money by leasing your air rights over your homestead.

Let's take an example that I had some personal experience in the Massachusetts Turnpike.

When I was getting my real estate license, the instructor went into great detail about everything I'm covering in this article. If you're familiar with the Big Dig, you know that it was a series of tunnels built beneath Boston to help with the traffic.

The air rights, despite the fact that they dug down, came into play. You own from your property to the core of the earth, too, all classified underneath the same set of rights. They paid $200m for air rights.

Air rights can be insanely expensive, and if the government seizes them for any purpose, under the fourteenth amendment, you would be a very rich man/woman. In a scenario like this, they could build on top of your real property, encroaching on your property in a most aggravating way.

In a case like this, I would reap compensation under the law and move to another household. Passive income, plenty of funding to prep an even better homestead.

# Chapter 4: Real Property

*"All land, structures, firmly attached and integrated equipment, anything growing on the land, and all "interests" in the property which may be the right to future ownership..."*
*– legal-dictionary.thefreedictionary.com*

To get a fully comprehensive guide on the definition of Real Property, view the video below.

Real property is not only the land itself but also all entities physically attached to it. The home, for example, is attached to the foundation; the foundation is attached to the ground. It's considered real property.

You may have heard a term, or read it somewhere when you bought your home, called Fee Simple. This states that you can leave your home, as defined by real property, to anyone you deem fit such as an heir or beneficiary, even if you're still paying a mortgage to your bank.

In this principle, the property is yours outright. While it's up for debate whether the government owns all banks or not, I'd like to see them pull a fast one on a third-party financial institution.

If your deed reads Fee Simple, gather the components of a will so there can be no dark attempts at stealing your land through nefarious means. By appointing a living heir, you're protecting your property from being taken by the government.

# Chapter 5: Mineral Rights

*"Referring to the ownership interest in minerals that are contained on or found under a particular parcel of land, irrespective of the ownership of the surface of the land."*
*– thelaw.com*

The United States is among the few countries that allow mineral rights in the first place. For the most part, every nation can claim gold and oil found six feet under your home.

Like I referenced earlier, if Jed lived in just about any other country, he'd still be another simpleton from the boonies with nothing to his name. It's laws like this that aid in capitalistic ideologies; anyone can be anything, especially if they strike it rich when trying to put in a custom hot tub three feet into the soil.

In order to best keep your mineral rights, whether it be for the purpose of excavating any precious metals or resources for your own point of sale, or leaving your land the way it is for future generations of your descendants to enjoy.

The choice is up to you, but if you notice there are valuable resources, contacting a lawyer about the whole ordeal should always be your first step.

# Chapter 6: Condemnation

Keep your home filthy to the point that sanitation is part of the question? Your home is prime for condemnation by the government. It could possibly serve hidden interests, but the most likely case scenario would be that the state-level government would be the ones condemning your home.

If you've been at the mercy of notices beforehand, or inspectors, and you're reading this because you're uncertain how to get your home ready in time, I'd recommend a maid service. Have them call in the big guns, and take a snow shovel to your belongings and fill up the dumpster.

Losing your home to condemnation is the most embarrassing way that the government can take your land.

# Chapter 7: Memorial Condemnation

After the events of September 11, 2001, the federal government tried to purchase the land in Pennsylvania where Flight 93 went down.

It took three years for the deal to be reached, awarding the landowners $9.5 million dollars, but if this was the case, why did it take more than three years to come to an agreement? This is because "Memorial Condemnation" is the unofficial name given to incidents just like these.

The gentleman who owns the lake where the tank of Space Shuttle Columbia was found in 2011 could end up being forced to sell. While it falls under the clause of eminent domain, and they have to provide compensation, there are no laws protecting your from their scrutiny and tactics to force a sale.

That's exactly what is believed to have happened with the Flight 93 space, and it's not all that far-fetched. You can retain your land but at the personal cost of your sanity.

# Chapter 8: Taxruptcy

This term refers to not paying your yearly property tax on your home or land. Your property tax is comprised of one percent of your Fair Market Value: the appraisal amount on your property, officially and for the books.

If your land is worth $100,000, you'll pay $1,000 yearly, and so on and so forth. Keep in mind that remodeling your home increases that yearly tax as well.

If the cost of your land suddenly jumps—as mentioned above under memorial condemnation—it could greatly affect your ability to remain on said land. If you're used to no more than $3,500 of yearly property tax, and the land is then appraised at $3,000,000 for whatever reason. (Archeological discovery of great importance, ruins found, graveyard, etc.) Then you'll be paying a whopping $30,000 per year on your home.

I don't know about you, but I sure can't afford that. It's just another tactic used by the government to legally steal your property. If you can't afford it, you'll either listen to their demands under eminent domain and receive proper compensation, or suffer the tax hike for as long as you can hack it. Trust me, they'll wait.

Here's a <u>resource</u> to validate any questions on 1% property tax.

# Conclusion

For each type of claim, use the following below to refuse the government possession of your property.

- **Eminent Domain** – Deny their movement
- **Surface Rights** – Read over and amend your deed if applicable
- **Air Rights** – Be careful about how you exercise the ability to lease your air space
- **Real Property** – It's tied down, it's bolted down; it's yours
- **Mineral Rights** – Seek assistance from a certified lawyer; this is the most common repo. Mineral rights are a right underneath any state in the United States of America. Whether or not they're included in the deed is the question we're trying to face.
- **Condemnation** – Fairly simple; keep your home up to above-par standards
- **Memorial Condemnation** – This is up in the air; not much can be done
- **Taxruptcy** – Pay your taxes, and if you can't, subdivide your land, pay less

These are all federal laws that all the states must follow. It is imperative you follow the federal laws that would prevent you from losing your property. Protect yourself with a bit of knowledge; under no other circumstances should the government attempt to repossess your property. Remember your rights; remember to exercise them properly, or you could be facing more than a backhoe in your backyard digging for gold.

## About the Author

Teresa has over 40 years of homesteading experience. She loves anything to do with living off the land on and off the grid. She believes in being self-sufficient. She raises her own foods, medicines, and crafts. Also, she is a really big fan of clean eating and pressure cooker recipes, as you can see within many of her different Homesteading series of books and e-books. Teresa specializes in and is a fan of Homesteading Skills which include raising meat rabbits, chickens, goats, hogs, cows, horses, ducks, poultry, and dogs, as well has all kinds of fruits, vegetables and herbs. She collects wild foods and hunts for what she doesn't raise on her small farm.

Teresa's homesteading series includes many book topics such as Home Brewing, slow cooker, clean eating, instant pot, crock pot, electric pressure cooker recipes, baking recipes, preserving, foraging, planting, building, and the list goes on.

Having a well-stocked pantry of easy to open and serve jars of food is essential for a busy family, whether farming, survival prepping, or just the normal city dweller. Follow Teresa to discover more about Homesteading Life Skills.

More about the Arden Marketing Enterprises at: Arden-ent.com

*Preview of*

## *'Fermented Foods for Gut Health'*

Discover the beneficial techniques of fermentation for a healthier gut!

In Fermented Foods for Gut Health, we will take you through the simple fermentation process, its benefits to your body.

With the scare of not using some form of antibacterial soap, sanitizers or pasteurized foods and dairy products, we are killing off not only the bad bacteria which is harmful to our bodies, but the good bacteria that is to our bodies for attaining optimum health too. It is a trend today to pay for expensive probiotic pills on eating huge amounts of yogurt to replace the good bacteria that are destroyed.

Many of the benefits include:

- Protects against pathogenic bacteria
- Improves digestion
- Helps your body to more effectively absorb nutrients from food
- Fermentation is a natural and safe method of food preservation, and doesn't involve any chemicals or artificial ingredients
- Not to mention it is easy and inexpensive to do

As the bacteria and yeast feed on sugars surrounding it, enzymes are released to break down the large food particles. In other words, fermented foods are predigested and it is full of enzymes, which the body needs.

Fermenting food is not a new concept. It has been around for thousands of years. Something that has been around that long has something to say about health. This is not just a way of preserving foods but also a way of eating healthier and having a healthier life.

Fermented Foods for Gut Health book will show you how to save some money while enjoying delicious ways to improve the gut flora for a better digestive system.

Click here to check out the rest of (Fermented Foods for Gut Health) on Amazon.

# Don't forget to check out Teresa's other books on Amazon.com.

Below you'll find some of my other books that are popular on Amazon and Kindle as well. Simply click on the links below to check them out. Alternatively, you can visit my author page on Amazon to see other work done by me.

Alkaline Diet Lifestyle: De-Alkaline Your Body for a Healthier Life

Fermented Foods for Gut Health: How Kimchi and Sauerkraut Can Improve Your Gut Health

Make Your Own Honey Mead at Home: The Homestead Series (Volume 2)

Brew Your Own Beer

The Burn Everything Cookbook: Stories and Recipe of Lean Times

Spirit Guides: Work and Bond with your Spirit Guide

How to Build a Moonshine Still plus recipes

If the links do not work, for whatever reason, you can simply search for these titles on the Amazon website to find them. Or try my Author page

# Coming Soon

*From my Homestead Series:*

How to Make Bannock Bread

How to Can Stews and Soups

Foraging in the Southern USA

How to Can Pork plus recipes

How to Can Beef plus recipes

How to Can Game plus recipes

If you have a great idea for a book, give us a call to discuss the next step to becoming an published Author.

# The End